mom~
spiration

Inspire Your Children to Pursue their Dreams
as You Pursue Your Own

mom~
spiration

Karla Marie Williams
Copyright 2019
ISBN 9781726845625

All Rights Reserved. No part of this book may be reproduced or transmitted in any form or by any means without permission from the author.

No part of this publication may be stored in a retrieval system, or transmitted in any form or by any means. Electronic, mechanical, photocopying, recording, or otherwise, without the permission of the publisher and author.

Publisher: iSpeak4KidsGlobal Publishing
Author: Karla Marie Williams
Language: English
Printed in the U.S.A.
First Edition

Table of Contents

Dedication		7
Introduction		10
mom~spiration #1	Example	15
mom~spiration #2	Dream	28
mom~spiration #3	Faith	45
mom~spiration #4	Smile	53
mom~spiration #5	Learn	63
mom~spiration #6	Give	73
mom~spiration #7	Integrity	83
mom~spiration #8	Mistakes	91
mom~spiration #9	Barriers	99
mom~spiration #10	Juggle	108
mom~spiration #11	Invest	116
mom~spiration #12	Sweat	125
mom~spiration #13	Order	134
mom~spiration #14	Fight	143
mom~spiration #15	Stand	154
mom~spiration #16	Win	162
mom~spiration #17	Re-Discover	171
mom~spiration #18	Gifts	178
Epilogue		184
Acknowledgements		187
Connect		188
Author's Work		189

Dedication

I dedicate this labor of love to my mother, Janet Marie Jewell (Trigg), 1944-2007.

Through mental illness, poverty, and insurmountable circumstances, you rose as a phoenix and overcame it all. You were a force to be reckoned with. You nurtured, raised, and exposed me to greatness. Your tenacity and refusal to give up have been a guiding light up to this very day.

You purchased our little piece of Heaven (home) in the middle of a drug and crime infested neighborhood, and turned it into a warm safe haven where we took refuge from the war going on outside our doors. You refused to go on welfare, and instead took every temporary job that came your way to keep our lives as consistent and joyful as you could.

You took me outside of our little world and exposed me to bigger things that helped me dream big dreams. You taught me about faith and unmoving hope. You showed me how to be comfortable in my own skin and celebrated me as I displayed my unique talents.

I can hear your infectious laughter that made for some of the most memorable childhood moments. I can also hear your sorrowful tears from yet another blow, problem, or seemingly impossible mountain; although you thought I was unaware.

Your latter years were filled with volunteering and giving of yourself and time to others. What an inspiration you were when you finished your degree at 58-years-old (38 years after beginning), just to prove you could.

I wish I could say that I listened to every lesson you tried to teach me. I wish I had taken the time to say thank you, and let you know how much your example and tenacity inspired me. Sometimes we don't get those lessons until much later in life. Mom, you inspired me, and continue to today. I pray I can do the same with my children. I pray through ups and downs, success and challenges that my life will speak louder than any words I could say. Thank you for letting me SEE your life and dreams! I miss you every day and I love you forever!

~Sugar Plum

Introduction

I had this Utopian view of being a mom long before I ever became one. The iconic mother that can do it all with a smile and a wave. I was going to be the poster child for the perfect wife and mom. My dream mom-self was amazing!

She was a sexy, vivacious, and supportive wife.
She was sweet, but not a pushover.
She was firm, but not a drill sergeant.
She was feminine, but didn't mind getting her hands dirty.
She was fashionable and always fit.
She was a masterful career woman.
She was president of the PTA.
She would never drive a mini-van.
She would cook healthy meals for her family every day.
She kept a spotless and luxurious home.
She threw amazing dinner parties.
She raised perfectly behaved children.
She traveled to exotic places with her family in tow.
She was a present and perfect friend.
She was a powerful and impactful minister.
She was a great leader and world changer.
She had it all, ALL AT ONCE…

I literally exhausted myself as I failed to meet all these expectations. It was not long into motherhood that I realized this woman I envisioned did not exist. Not for me. Not for anyone. The best advice I was given before I became a mom was this: "You can have it all. You just cannot have it all at the same time, in the same season of life." That statement changed my life and gave me grace for every single season that was to follow. I have been able to be THAT MOM at different seasons of my life, but I have not been able to be THAT MOM all at once. I can be who my children need me to be in each season of their lives, and allow my life to inspire them.

As the years have gone by, motherhood, as I have known it, has inspired my dreams and God-given journey. In return, pursuing my dreams has inspired my children to pursue their own.

I encourage you to believe in yourself, your dreams, and God's ability to bring them to pass. You have on the inside of you the gifts to impact the world and I want to inspire you to let them loose. Momma, you CAN fly and you can take your family along for the flight.

My purpose for writing this book is to AWAKEN, INSPIRE, and PUSH moms to think big and remember their dreams in the midst of mom-life. I want to help reawaken your vision that has the ability to inspire your family while propelling YOU to another level.

You may not be able to be all things, all the time. However, you can allow each season of your life to inspire your children. Let's give our kids some mom~spiration and take them on the journey with us as we soar to new heights!

"It's not only children who grow. Parents do too. As much as we watch to see what our children do with their lives, they are watching us to see what we do with ours. I cannot tell my children to reach for the sun. All I can do is reach for it, myself."
Joyce Maynard

mom~spiration #1

Let Them See an Example

"Her children stand and bless her. Her husband praises her..."
Proverbs 31:28 NLT

*H*ave you ever felt like you did not measure up to this Proverbs 31 woman? Have you ever felt like you did not measure up to society's expectations of you as a mom? How have other's opinions affected how you live, parent, and pursue your dreams?

The mommy wars put working moms and stay-at-home moms against each other in a fight for who and what is best. We cannot base our family, our choices, or our dreams on the opinions of people that are not vested in the future of our family.

Since so many people point out the perfection in the Proverbs 31 woman and how focused she was on taking care of her family, I decided to look a little closer. What would it tell me about her? What would it tell me about myself and my role as a mom?

I have been told by many that pursuing anything outside of my home and family is selfish. I was even told by one well-meaning mother that the purpose of a mother is simply that – to mother; nothing else.

This example in Proverbs shares something entirely different, if we dissect it properly.

Proverbs 31 NLT

v13   She finds wool and flax and busily spins it.

v14   She is like a merchant's ship, bringing her food from afar.

v15 She gets up before dawn to prepare breakfast for her household and plan the day's work for her servant girls.

v16 She goes to inspect a field and buys it; with the earnings she plants a vineyard.

v17 She is energetic and strong, a hard worker.

v18 She makes sure her dealings are profitable; her lamp burns late into the night.

v19 Her hands are busy spinning thread, her fingers twisting fiber.

v20 She extends a hand to the poor and opens her hand to the needy.

v24 She makes belted linen garments and sashes to sell to the merchants.

v26 When she speaks her words are wise, and she gives instructions with kindness.

v27 She carefully watches everything in her household and suffers nothing from laziness.

When reading the highlighted verses mentioned, I have come to several conclusions. Not only does this woman esteem and care for her husband, she also cares for her household and children well. She is an enterprising entrepreneur and an employer. She is wise, generous, kind, and talented. She values her talents and markets them well. She believes that what she has to offer is desirable. She works hard day and night to perfect her craft all while caring for her home.

Think about her kids and the enterprising example she set for them. I am quite positive that she involved them in the creating, marketing, and selling of her fine products. They saw her working day and night to create beautiful garments. I am sure they were also involved in the planting and harvesting of the vineyard she purchased. If you read the entire chapter you can see that her husband was confident and proud of the work that his wife did. He was not worried about whether she could handle her household, the kids, and entrepreneurial pursuits. She is the ultimate example.

> "Children learn more from what you are than what you teach."
> W.E.B. Du Bois

Do not let society, friends, family, a church, or complete strangers define motherhood for you. Whether you are a single mom, stay-at-home mom, working mom, or work-at-home mom, your purpose, dreams, and passions are important. You should not be made to feel guilty for pursuing them. Go for it girl! Write that book, start that business or organization, go for the promotion, start that blog, go back to school, volunteer, create, and display all the beauty and talent God has given you.

Living Vicariously

It is easy to find yourself living vicariously through your children. It is even easier to see your friends or favorite social media personality live their best life while you are cheering from the sidelines.

You know there is purpose and destiny that brews right below the surface in you as you change diapers, fix lunches, help with homework, and go to PTA meetings. Every season of motherhood is important. Be patient, love those babies and know God has a timing for everything.

In my book Homeschool Gone WILD, I share about parents who live vicariously through their children. They want their children to pursue things they never did. Our children are individuals and need the room to be themselves. The best way to inspire them is not through control, but by pursuing our own dreams.

"When our dreams and passions come AFTER everything and everyone else, the dreams turn into a pile of regrets."

Over the years, my children have accomplished things I am very proud of, however, those are their accomplishments, not mine. There is a fine line between supporting our children's dreams and taking them on as our own.

Do Your Kids Know You?

Do your children know you? I mean, do they REALLY know you outside of your role as a mother? Do they know what you wanted to be when you grew up? Have you shared your dreams and goals with them?

> "Sometimes the greatest adventure is simply a conversation."
> Amadeus Wolfe

Have you shared details of your life before motherhood with them - your experiences, jobs, education, and travels? Do they know what inspires you and makes your heart skip a beat? Your mistakes, failures, and successes can propel them into their dreams. What makes you happy, excited, or sad? Do they know?

Naturally, we want our children to see us as flawless. That should not be the goal. Our children need to know we are human. They need to know we have faults, needs, dreams, and have questions just like they do. This helps them to understand reality and not perfection. Certainly not a Hollywood or reality TV version of themselves.

Who are you REALLY? Not the roles that you play, but the person. I encourage you to not just get to know your children, but to let them really get to know you. Open up and let them into your world outside of motherhood.

Do What I Say, Not What I Do?

I conducted a survey on three social media platforms of 25-60 year olds. I asked the question:

Did you learn more from your parents by listening to what they told you? Or did you learn more from your parents by watching how they lived their lives? Eighty-eight percent of those that responded said that they learned more from their parents by watching them live rather than any words they said.

This revelation was astounding to me. I am guilty of telling my kids a lot of things. Dare I admit that I have been a serial lecturer in the past? I am learning to do more living in front of them instead of lecturing these days. I have come to the conclusion that my children learn the most impactful life lessons by what is caught rather than what is taught.

This does not mean that I do not have crucial conversations with my children. It means that I need to live what I am teaching if I really want it to impact their lives.

Retroactive Wisdom

You may think that your kids don't listen to you anyway, so why put all this energy into trying to inspire them. Maybe you feel you have not been much of an inspiration and find it hard to dig yourself out of that parenting ditch. I get it!

There have been times when I felt like my current state could not possibly be beneficial to anyone around me. As parents we are not batting a thousand all of the time. No one expects us to.

Inspiring your children is more about the life you live. So stand tall and live well. Pursue big things right in front of them and make them a part of the pursuit.

I have a memory of an interaction with my mother that I wish I could forget. It breaks my heart how cold and insensitive I was to her as a teenager.

One day after school she asked if I would like to tag along with her on an appointment she had that evening. My response: "I will be glad when you get a real job. It is so embarrassing to tell my friends that my mom sells vacuum cleaners door-to-door!" With tears in her eyes, she left without responding.

I didn't get it. I could not see the lessons in what she was doing. My pride got in the way of appreciating how hard she worked to provide for us. Today, I see it as clear as day. I like to call it retroactive wisdom. It is wisdom that is gained in hindsight and comes with maturity and life experience. The lessons she lived out loud for me and the inspiration I pull from her today are priceless.

> "I have been perfectly designed and assigned by God to be the mom my kids need."
> Lysa Terkeurst

A child's vision is limited. Their life experience only gives them a snippet of an entire situation. Let your life shine. They may not get it today, but they will get it. Expose them to greatness and the path toward your dreams anyway. The choices you make and the dreams you pursue today will inspire them in the future.

"I like to call it retroactive wisdom. It is wisdom that is gained in hindsight and comes with maturity and life experience."

Family Affair

Often times we feel guilty about pursuing things we are passionate about because we feel like it is going to take away from our family. We must look at our dreams as a part of our family vision. When you include your family and make it a family affair, the way you approach it will lend more liberty and confidence.

> "All our dreams can come true, if we have the courage to pursue them."
> Walt Disney

Whether it is going back to school, starting a new business, traveling around the world, volunteering for a cause, or anything else you are dreaming of, make it inclusive. This does not mean everyone in the family has to be passionate about the same things. It simply means that you have to build it into your life and not separate it.

I spend a lot of time learning new things. As I demonstrate that willingness to dive into new and foreign topics or experiences, my children watch and join in. It also develops a resolute and demanding desire within them to know more, do more, and experience more of the world around them. They learn from watching their parents do it.

Define Success for Yourself

What is success? Is it the accumulation of wealth and things? Or is it much deeper than that? How will I know I have attained it?

"We must look at our dreams as a part of our family vision."

For one mom, success may mean being the CEO of a multi-million dollar empire. For another, it may mean opening her own local bakery. Another mom may find success in volunteering or caring for the elderly as her passion.

We cannot allow others to define success for us. We must define it for ourselves and not be moved by someone else's definition. This will encourage our children to do the same.

What do kids learn by watching our example?

- ❖ They pick up on our habits.
- ❖ They pick up on our moods, feelings, and outlooks on life.
- ❖ They learn how to navigate the world by watching us.

mom~spiration #2

Let Them

See You

Dream

"If you don't have a dream there is no way to make one come true."
Steven Tyler

*B*eing a mom and having a dream can co-exist. What passions have you laid down in the name of motherhood martyrdom? As mothers we are constantly guarding the hearts of our children and imparting words of encouragement. We know they are unique and have talents the world can benefit from. However, we don't believe that for ourselves. We are also unique and gifted in many ways that can be a blessing to the world around us. As parents, we owe it to our children to go for big things with the same gusto we encourage them to.

You may be saying to yourself that there is nothing about you or what you do that can possibly be an inspiration to your kids. You may have even compared yourself to the snippets of lives you see on social media. Heads up momma! The life you live in front of your kids will have an impact on them and future generations. You have wisdom, experiences, expertise, and gifts that can inspire them to be their very best.

Many of our children will see the sacrifices and the work that we do to help them achieve their dreams as it is happening around them. It may take others far into adulthood to appreciate everything their parents did to nurture, encourage, and facilitate an environment for the foundation of the dreams they live as an adult. Whether they say thank you, notice your efforts today, or 25 years from now, you owe it to yourself to push toward your dreams and in turn inspire your children.

I can hear all the excuses because I have made them myself. When the kids are grown, I will write my book. When I have more money, I will start my business. When I lose weight, I will have more confidence to get my dream job. Our lists can go on and on until finally, we give up on our passion altogether.

You might have pushed all your dreams and interests to the background. Life has thrown so many curve balls your way, you are afraid to dream. Don't be! Dream openly, boldly, and courageously in front of your children.

God created YOU to do something that no other person on the face of this earth can do. Remember God's divine purpose for you, inclusive of motherhood. You are not doing yourself, or your children any favors by pretending that being a mom is your only purpose in life. Somebody, somewhere is depending on you to do what God has called you to do.

Seasons

There are seasons and timings for everything. It is important to know what season of life you are in, and take advantage of that season to the fullest. If we are not in a season of doing or pursuing our dreams, then we are in the season of preparation. Even in a season of preparation our children are able to learn a lot from us. I believe we can have it all. Just not all at the same time, or in the same season.

I have been through many seasons in my life as a mother. I waited a long time to become a mom. My dream was to stay home and care for my children. Multiple times since I have been a mother, I have tried to work outside the home. It just was not a fit for me. I have been a stay-at-home mom, a working mom, and now a work-at-home mom. Every season has had it's blessings and challenges, but every season has been special.

I don't regret the early years of diapering, cuddling, and soothing babies. That is such a special time for children and for moms. If this is the season you are in, enjoy it, cherish it, and be your best right where you are.

There have been other seasons of my life where I have struggled with my role as a mom and the passions that stir within me. My husband and I were ordained ministers and extremely active in a large church for close to twenty years. When our first three children were adopted we were leaders of multiple areas of ministry. For some reason we really thought becoming parents of three children over night would be a piece of cake. It was not, by a long shot. I struggled daily with all of my ministerial responsibilities and the needs of my children. I was not the mom that I wanted to be during that season of life.

It did not take long for my husband and I to decide to withdraw from many of our obligations and later resign completely. It was frowned upon by a lot of people. It was a decision we had to make based on our priority and season of life. I will never regret that decision. My children's needs were more important than anyone else's at that time. I firmly believe that my home is my first ministry.

I am the mom of six inspired kids who are reaching for their dreams. My husband and I continually pursue our passions. It has just become part of the atmosphere. When we are fulfilled in our purpose, we are happier people and better parents. I am a happier mom because I realized God's call on my own life. I am able to share that with my children. As long as my marriage and home are my first priority, pursuing my passion is a good thing!

Let them see your list of goals and vision boards. Display them proudly for the whole family to see. Talk about them. Pray together about them. Go see things that encourage them. The more you do this, the more your dreams will influence your children's view of their own.

Dreaming Big

Looking back over my life, I can remember one deep, passionate yearning. There is only one way to describe my childhood dreams. I wanted to CHANGE THE WORLD. The young Karla wanted to bring smiles to sad faces and hope to hopeless hearts. I know that sounds like a cliché, but it is the truth. That was it. That dream took on several forms over the years, but one thing remained consistent. Whatever I did, I wanted it to positively impact other's lives in a meaningful and lasting way.

I notice as I get closer and closer to the dreams that God has placed on my heart, He gives me more pieces to the puzzle. He enlarges the dream. The expansiveness of the dreams become so large, they seem impossible to attain on my own.

In 2007, I decided to be a stay-at-home mom after a successful career in banking and human resource management. It took a couple of years to adjust to the at-home life, but it is a choice that I would make all over again. A few years later, we began homeschooling. Being home took on an entirely new look. It was all-consuming. You can read more about our inspired homeschool journey in my first book, "Homeschool Gone WILD".

I began to notice myself get a little antsy. I wanted to be home with my kids, but I also wanted to experience the thrill of "personal" success. I was surrounded by friends who were climbing corporate ladders. I also had lots of at-home friends that were content with being home. I was in the middle. I had a yearning for something more, but I did not want to give up the freedom and joy that came from being home with my children.

I would like to tell you my story of how one vague dream turned into an international mission…and a DREAM COME TRUE!

After adopting our six children (two sibling groups of three), I came to the realization that there was a huge gap missing in the process for prospective foster/adoptive families. Many families were unprepared and ill-equipped for traumatized children. The romanticized adoption process took a front seat to preparation and education that were causing families to have rougher than necessary transitions, and increased adoption disruptions. I was also seeing an increase in Secondary Trauma (parents and siblings traumatized by the behavior of a child) in foster and adoptive parents as a result of the lack of preparation, education, and support. This needed to change. Kid's lives and the health of families depended on it.

Learning what I had learned from parenting and educating myself on trauma competency, I began a blog in 2010 at the advice of a dear friend. I had never written on the topic before. I just knew I needed to start somewhere. It was not an instant success. I wrote my heart out for all three of my followers. I could have easily stopped there and simply recorded my experiences and wisdom. I couldn't. There was something bigger on the inside of me.

I began to seek out ways to share my passion. This led to being a guest on a few radio shows. Shortly after appearing on one of the programs, I received an offer to become a radio host of my own show, Family by Design Radio. Again, a new experience that was pretty frightening, but I decided to walk through the door. Having never done anything like this before, I made lots of mistakes.

I interviewed over 40 guests and educated 1000-1700 listeners a month from the perspectives of adoptees, foster alumni, adoptive parents, birth parents, child welfare professionals, ethical missionaries, authors, celebrities, and more. This was a platform that took me by surprise and I really did not know where it would lead.

I recorded my radio program in my closet (on a broke down laptop) every Tuesday morning in Michigan for a radio station in Texas. I accomplished this while PBS Kids and goldfish crackers babysat my kids in the next room. I could have waited for a more sophisticated production system, but my dream was calling. Sometimes you just have to go with what you have at the time. There will NEVER be a perfect scenario.

The kids will never be the perfect age. Your finances may never be perfect. We can find any number of things that could be potential roadblocks in the way of pursuing something new. Just start. Things tend to fall into place when you are inspired and driven by a lifelong dream.

Soon I found myself on the stage at conferences, advocating for the needs of vulnerable children all over the United States. I trained foster and adoptive parents and social workers in caring for traumatized children. I volunteered at many of the events just to establish a voice and expertise in the field. It worked! I enjoyed taking my children to these events. They had the opportunity to see what I do and my heart for others.

I sat on panels and spoke alongside professionals with an entire alphabet of credentials next to their name. In the beginning this was intimidating, having only had two years of college. Once I found my voice, dove into self-study, and developed my expertise and platform, all those insecurities began to subside.

> *"Dream openly, boldly, and courageously in front of your children."*

My children were able to witness this transition from dream to fruition. They saw the late nights of me preparing materials and presentations. They heard the discussions between myself and my husband on the vision, direction, and goals for our new organization iSpeak4KidsGlobal. We shared our plans and the outcome of our work with them.

In 2014, I was asked to join the board of an international child welfare organization. This organization is impacting the lives of children and families all over the globe, and I have a front row seat to experience it. This was a game changer.

Later that year, I had the opportunity to travel to Ethiopia and Ghana with the organization. It would be my very first international audience and training. My kids watched as I prepared for this new experience by studying history, cultures, languages, customs, currency, and the geography of the countries I was scheduled to visit. Some of the dreams my kids have today have been inspired by the travel and international work I have done.

After returning from Ethiopia and Ghana, I began to get requests to train and consult in other countries through my own organization. Training, professional development, and consultations in Zimbabwe, Malawi, South Africa, Thailand, Costa Rica, Mexico, and India followed over the next five years.

I was able to impact children and families, promote trauma competent care, individually mentor parents, and build long lasting relationships all over the globe. It has been a whirlwind dance. Experiencing different cultures, languages, food, wildlife, and environments was just the icing on the cake.

There were many struggles along the way. There was the mommy-guilt, funding issues, logistical nightmares in other countries, terrorist scares, technology fails, Visa issues, and more.

Every single time that I was preparing to leave the country, something completely absurd would happen with one of the kids, or our finances. It would add to my mom-guilt and have me questioning myself all over again. Why was I doing this? Am I being selfish? Is God in this? Will my family be OK? Where will this lead me? I thank God for my husband, who has always kept me focused and encouraged me to continue the work that I do in the face of so many things that try to distract me from the dream.

We have developed a lifestyle over the last five years that has worked well for our family. We homeschool our children and that is my priority at this season in my life. I am able to travel a few times a year internationally and do a few local/regional trainings in my home state. This allows me to pursue my passion and focus on my family. My husband has been able to keep his schedule flexible to be present when I am out of the country. Pursuing things in the right season can make all the difference.

I recall another season over the last few years that required me to reconsider my goals. I was moving fast and had a lot of offers to speak around the country and outside the US. After returning from Malawi, Africa, I decided to cancel all of my engagements, for the rest of the year. God made it very clear to me to spend the year on my family. After sharing this with my husband we planned the rest of the year vacationing and doing activities with our kids.

God always knows how to direct you during every season of your life. It is up to you to listen and obey His guidance. That year was pivotal for our family in bonding and rebuilding sibling relationships.

You may ask, "How do I know what season I am in?" We have always determined our season in prayer taking into account the needs of our children and household. We never make a decision without being in agreement. Our dreams are interwoven.

I am still dreaming. I want to touch the lives of millions of children by advocating for family reunification. I want to empty orphanages and advocate for family based care across the US and the globe. I will not stop, and I am taking my children along with me on this journey. I want them to see the world and experience what I do first hand.

Why did I share all of this with you? I know that moms everywhere are dreaming. I know that we wait "until" to do anything about it. What are you waiting for? I am here to tell you that you don't have to wait.

> *"Pursuing things in the right season can make all the difference."*

Sometimes we stop dreaming because we have a hard time seeing through our present day scenario. How am I going to start a business with toddlers under foot? How am I going to go back to school with a new baby? After the kids grow up? After they graduate from college? After I lose weight? After I have more money saved? After I find my dream job? Then I will be happy. When our dreams and passions come AFTER everything and everyone else, the dreams turn into a pile of regrets.

Many times the dreams we have are intricately connected to our family. I have seen and witnessed the dreams God has placed on the heart of my children even at a young age; they are interwoven with my husband and myself in many ways. No matter the age of your children, you can include them in your pursuits. Whether they are five years old or twenty-five, go on this journey together.

Big dreams may seem unrealistic. They require you to trust God, trust yourself, and put your trust in others to help you along the way.

The key is recognizing where our dreams come from. We must abandon the dreams forced upon us by others and embrace the ones God has placed on the inside of us. That longing that just won't go away. He put it there!

When we learn how to identify and pursue our dreams, we teach our kids how to do the same. I challenge you to step out into unchartered territory holding your dream in one hand and your children in the other.

What do children learn from watching you dream?

- ❖ They train their eyes to look past the present.
- ❖ They see their dreams as significant and worthy of pursuit.
- ❖ They become excited about who they are and their individual gifts and talents.
- ❖ They value others' dreams as much as they do their own.

Dream Builder

Don't allow your dreams to stay in your head or in the past. Solidify what you are trying to pursue by giving it a vision. Create a vision statement that represents what you are passionate about and what attaining it will look like for you. (Refer to mom~spiration #17)

mom~spiration:
Dream Together

Spend a day or weekend dreaming with your family. Share your dreams with them and listen to their dreams. You can do this in the form of a journal, a video, vision boards or simple conversations. Make it a special time without distractions.

mom~spiration #3

Let Them

See

Your Faith

"I can do all things through Christ who strengthens me."
Philippians 4:13

*L*et them see your faith! I gave my life to Christ when I was fifteen years old. I never turned back. My faith has only grown and matured over the years. My relationship with God was a very personal thing. I have always longed for private prayer and worship to refuel.

When I became a mom, I remained very private when it came to my prayer time and Bible study. My husband was the one who openly prayed and read his Bible in front of the kids. I realized that my children did not see me doing this.

Once I realized that, I began changing how, when, and where I spent my God-time. I made sure that our conversations highlighted God's thoughts regarding our everyday life.

I have never been strict when it comes to sharing my faith. I always felt it was better for our children to see our faith rather than it be forced upon them; with the risk of chasing them in the opposite direction.

I remember my mom's subtle ways of sharing her faith without being pushy or overbearing. All throughout my childhood there was theme music in our home. Family Life Radio's talk programs, music, and messages were on 24/7. As a teenager, it became irritating and convicting. Later in life it has become a sweet memory of her faith and her living it out loud in front of us. It was a seed that has bloomed into something beautiful in my adulthood.

"Many things are more caught than taught; faith is one of them."

Not only did I want my kids to witness my daily routine. I wanted them to see how I develop my relationship with God. I wanted them to know how to trust God as well. I remind my kids often of how blessed we are and point out the things God has done for all of us.

I am not in favor of planting seeds of worry or fear in our children when things get tough or we are going through difficult times. Our emphasis is always on helping them use their faith toward the end goal or need. We point out and help them see God moving in that situation every step of the way. What we try to do is frame our challenges as something that can be overcome by faith in our God who can, has, and will deliver us out of any situation. When we see these victories, we celebrate them with our children. We point them back to the one who cares about every aspect of our lives.

He cares about our family, relationships, health, finances, and jobs. Believe it or not He cares about our dreams too. Yes! God cares about your dreams. The dreams that are undeniable, the gifts that are unexplainable, and the drive to show His glory through us was placed there by Him. Of course He wants them to come to pass!

I am very intentional about helping my children see God in their gifts and talents. I want them to trust Him to bring those dreams to pass and to live their faith out loud in whatever area they shine. Believe God together for things that your family needs and desires. Identify when you see God working in the situation. Celebrate together when the manifestation presents itself.

For many years, I prayed and talked about traveling the world and being a blessing to others. I would talk to my children about it all the time, not knowing how and when any of this would materialize. They celebrated along the journey as we watched God orchestrate some pretty amazing things and literally take our vision international. They were able to see the outcome of their faith and prayer because I involved them in that process.

Let them see your faith! Live your faith out loud for them to catch. Many things are more caught than taught; faith is one of them.

What do children learn from watching you live out your faith?

- ❖ They recognize that He has a plan for their lives.
- ❖ They learn how to trust God to bring His plan to pass in their lives.
- ❖ They learn how to lean on God during the hard times and push through road blocks that stand between themselves and their dreams.

Dream Builder

Sometimes we can exercise our faith by rehearsing our past victories. Write down the past victories that you have had that fuel your faith for your current pursuits.

---

mom~spiration:
Share your faith

Spend time with your children sharing how exercising your faith has impacted your life. Ask them how faith has impacted their lives and what they have learned.

mom~spiration #4

Let Them See You Smile

"The future belongs to those who believe in the beauty of their dreams."
Eleanor Roosevelt

*H*appy wife, happy life! How many times have we heard this phrase? The same is true with children. Joyful mom, joyful kids! As moms we set the temperature for our home. Much of the mood and environment in our home depends on us.

There are scores of moms that are unhappy. They feel they have lost themselves in a sea of diapers, toys, and doctor appointments. The dreams they had are hidden away in a closet begging to be released and set free.

We find ourselves punchy, short, irritable, and even angry at the shadows of our dreams taunting us from years gone by. Shake off the stressors that are keeping you from enjoying life and pursuing new things.

I found myself living in a constant state of stress. Stressed about money, kids, health, ministry, extended family, and everything in between. When I came to the conclusion that I cannot control any of these things, I was finally able to release the worry to God. This opened up my heart and mind to joy and focusing on the life that I wanted to live instead of everything that could go wrong.

We have been lied to and deceived into thinking that we cannot pursue things outside of motherhood and it causes restlessness and discomfort. You know that the passion is there. Every now and then a picture, song, commercial, or conversation will remind you of what you once dreamed of.

"Only as high as I reach can I grow, only as far as I seek can I go, only as deep as I look can I see, only as much as I dream can I be."
Karen Raun

This may be a bold statement but I will say it anyway. <mark>Stop using your kids as an excuse to remain unhappy and unfulfilled</mark>. Instead, allow them to be an inspiration of child-like faith. You owe it to yourself and your children to be joyful and to pursue the things that set your heart on fire.

They need to see you smile, laugh, and enjoy life. The feeling of walking toward and accomplishing God's purpose for your life brings great joy. Joy is contagious. It rubs off on your children and gives them a glimpse of the real you.

I have allowed disappointment in my lack of achievement to affect the mood that I set in my home. There was a time when I felt that having six kids meant my dreams had become impossible. It led to anger and the resentment of the very kids God blessed me with.

"Stop today and give thanks that God has given you what you once prayed desperately for."
Alli Worthington

I would see other people traveling, getting dream jobs, and making their mark on the world while I was changing diapers and teaching yet another child to read. As a result, there was not much positive modeling going on from my end. I was counting down the days until the last child turned 18. I was miserable and overwhelmed. You could not see it though. I was good at faking it.

Do men experience this too's hide it? Or do moms just allow Dads to have more balance?

Can I just be real? My attitude stunk. It was a privilege to be home with my kids and connect with them on an intimate level at their age. What was I thinking? How could I look at motherhood that way? I was in a precious season and I needed to cherish it. I realized being a mom was one of the greatest gifts I have ever received. I was making my mark on the world through my children. Recognizing this brought me joy and in turn changed the environment in my home.

God still had a purpose for me in the midst of all my mothering. He did not change His mind. Becoming a mom did not cancel out my destiny. It has not canceled yours.

It took a real attitude adjustment, prayer, and boldness to step out and trust that I could accomplish God's purpose for my life; even in the midst of my most important role as a mom. I had to rid myself of unnecessary stress, and trust God to lead me in His timing.

Once I gained perspective I was able to enjoy life and my family again. The joy on my kid's faces when I sit down to talk, play a game, joke around, or even do my famous dance moves, is worth a million dollars. Whatever your circumstance or stage of dream fulfillment, do not forget to have fun and smile with your family. Those will be the moments they remember the most.

Sometimes you have to practice joyfulness consciously until it becomes natural. You may have to do some things on purpose to reinvent your outlook on life and the beauty around you.

"Joy is contagious. It rubs off on your children and gives them a glimpse of the real you."

I can remember years ago when I was so uptight that I fussed about everything. I was always on edge. One day the kids knew I was gonna fly off the handle about the massive mess they made making a fort out of the entire family room. Instead, I climbed right into the fort and began role playing as one of the super heroes. They responded in shock, which soon turned to laughter and joy. I have learned to do that more and more as they have gotten older. It keeps things light hearted and stress free.

What happened when I had a change in focus and attitude? Joy happened. That unbelievable feeling that I was right where I was supposed to be at each moment. There is nothing that can compare to the happiness that comes from knowing you are following God's call and dream He planted in you. Not a manufactured dream, but His dream.

The joy you experience from setting those dreams free will flood your home and onto your family. I love being a mom. I also love being able to share my true interests and passions with my kids. It is the best of both worlds.

Play with your kids. Relax and let yourself enjoy little moments. Take joy in the small and big things. Joy is contagious!

What does your joy teach your children?

- ❖ They learn that you can be joyful when everything is not perfect.
- ❖ They learn that being in the middle of God's will for their life brings joy.
- ❖ They learn how to define happiness for themselves.

Dream Builder

Stress affects the way we approach our dreams and can steal our joy. Identify the major stressors in your life and make a plan to respond differently or eliminate them altogether.

mom~spiration:
Have Fun Together

Plan a fun-filled day or evening with your children away from any stress, work, or daily pressures. Smile, laugh, and have fun together as you appreciate them for the blessing that they are. Make this a regular habit.

mom~spiration #5

Let Them See You Learn

"You are never too old to set another goal or to dream a new dream."
Unknown

*W*hat are you actively learning right now? We are not talking about life lessons here. When is the last time you set out on an adventure to learn something new, or master a new skill?

Our children need to see us continually evolving. Involving them in the evolution of our knowledge and experiences gives them a clear picture of what it takes to gain new skills and see that learning never stops.

"A classroom does not need to have four walls."
Unknown

I met a person a few years back that said to me, "I have not read a book in 15 years." You can imagine how shocked I was. When you are inspired, you are always looking for new knowledge and motivation.

I was inspired to be a life-long learner by my mom. My dear mother started college when she was 20 years old. After my oldest brother was born, she put her education on the back burner. After having three children and later a divorce, her focus was on survival and taking care of us. There was not much time or money for college. What I do remember is that she did not let that stop her from learning and growing.

I observed my mother learn, perfect, and market her skills as an executive secretary. The skills she had developed were in-demand at that time. She was one of the fastest typists and transcriptionist in short-hand in our area.

If you were born after the 1980's, you may not know what short-hand is. It is an abbreviated language of symbols that allow for lightning fast note taking; very similar to a combination of the text language of today and hieroglyphics. She was in high-demand in courts and city/county office meetings because of her skills.

Although it was rare for my mom to find a permanent job, due to mental illness, she developed and rocked her skills. Those skills paid for our little piece of Heaven on Alma Street and hamburgers at McDonalds every other Friday.

Later, she went on to complete her degree at the age of 58. She did not have a career progression in mind. She simply wanted to accomplish that goal. This taught us so much about tenacity and the willingness to always remain teachable.

> "There are two educations. One should teach us how to make a living and the other how to live."
> John Adams

Following my mother's example, I realized that I had a lot to learn to pursue the dreams that I had. I went to conferences that focused on child welfare. On-line classes that focused on global justice and child welfare were very helpful to me. I took in as much information as I could. My own personal experience was not enough to become an expert in the field.

I found people who were at the forefront of ethical missions and child welfare all over the world. Even hosting my own radio program was a learning process as I interviewed and gained knowledge from the best.

I soaked up every book I could get my hands on that discussed trauma and tragedy. I learned how it affects the brain development, relational skills, and future of a child that does not experience intervention and compassion. I made it my mission to study the best ways of caring for and nurturing children that have lived through horrific things, starting with my own.

I did not return to college in a traditional sense. However, I took every opportunity to understand everything that related to my topic of interest.

I did not do this off to the side or in the absence of my children. I did it right in front of them. I involved them. I discussed what I was learning and helped them see the passion and vision I had for making a difference in this area. They recognize through these examples of seeing us learn that learning does not have an expiration date. They have observed the fact that being open to learn something new at any age can propel their lives forward into new and exciting adventures.

> *"My husband and I don't want to experience our dreams without our children by our side."*

We develop an environment in our home where learning is a natural daily pursuit for all of us. The way we chose to unconventionally educate our children through unschooling reflects this. We dive into the things they are interested in and we involve them in our pursuits as parents.

Speaking of limitless learning, this reminds me of my father-in-love. When my husband was in high school, his father decided he wanted to better his career and try something new. He applied for a job that was outside of his expertise and skill. That did not stop him at all. He sent my husband to the library to get all the books he could find on the topic of horticulture, grounds keeping, and gardening. He hadn't done anything like this before. His drive to better himself financially and learn caused him to study a new industry. He got the job and spent the next 25 years doing something that brought him joy and increased his family in many ways.

My husband often talks about how much that taught him. These lessons have been reflected in his willingness to take risks and go for new and out-of-the-box dreams; many of which he has accomplished. He would not have learned much at all if his father did not involve him in that pursuit and dream. He would have benefited, but may have never picked up on those crucial lessons.

As I continually travel and expand my vision for iSpeak4KidsGlobal, I keep my kids by my side for the ride. When I took my oldest daughter to Zimbabwe we spent months together learning bits and pieces of the local language, the country's history, culture, and the orphan crisis. My oldest son will accompany me on my next trip to Malawi. We are beginning to delve into language, culture, and studying everything we want to learn about the country.

When I take my kids to conferences with me in and outside the country, I make sure they are present during the training. They assist me with materials and logistics as well as learn a lot about public speaking along the way. Each time we visit a new state or country, we plan a few adventures outside of business to explore. This allows us to take in the culture and beauty of our surroundings. Whether I am preaching at a tiny church in a village, or my daughter is chasing wildebeests through the Zimbabwean bush, or experiencing local museums, we are dreaming, learning, growing, and enjoying life together. My husband and I don't want to experience our dreams without our children by our side.

It is a goal for our entire family to travel globally together. Until that comes to fruition, we take each of our children away for an adventure to broaden their vision and perspective of this beautiful world we live in.

What do children learn by watching their parents continually pursue knowledge?

- ❖ Learning never stops.
- ❖ It is never too late.
- ❖ You can master a new skill at any age.
- ❖ Knowledge brings expertise.
- ❖ Expertise can increase you financially.

Dream Builder

What do you need to learn to become an expert in an area you are pursuing? Do research to find classes, books, experts, and information on your area of passion.

mom~spiration:
Learn Together

Swap learning experiences with your kids. Take part in learning something they are interested in. Dive into the topic or skill with them. Then involve them in learning something that you love. Give them a chance to experience something new through your eyes. Have this learning exchange often.

mom~spiration #6

Let Them See You Give

"Give. Even when you know you can get nothing back."
Yasmin Mogahed

I am sure you would agree with me when I say that I want my children to be givers. I desire that they seek to be a blessing to others. I pray they use their gifts and talents to improve the lives of people in many ways, wherever they go, and whatever they do.

It is very difficult to have that goal and not be a giver ourselves, isn't it? Of course, I want my children to be paid well for the work that they do and appreciated in that way. It does not have to be an either or situation. You can excel financially and be a giver.

As a matter of fact, I think we do our children a disservice when we teach them that the world revolves around them. We don't help them by teaching that things are more important than people. The best thing we could give them is sharing the compassion and fulfillment that comes from giving and caring about the needs of others.

My mother was a living example of giving for me growing up. We had very little to share, yet she still found ways to give. Whether it was offering a temporary place to stay, clothes, food, or even money, she knew something that many people don't know about giving. She knew that she was receiving much more than the person who benefited from her generosity. You don't have to be wealthy to be a giver, you just have to care.

Watching my mom's example gave me a heart to love people and to give in multiple ways. Giving does not always have to be financial. Giving of your time, talent, resources, favor, and money can change a person's life at just the right moment.

Early in our marriage we gave away two vehicles to people who desperately needed them. We did not do it for praise, nor did we do it to get anything in return. Our lives, however, have been abundantly blessed as a result of our determination to be a blessing to others. My children have witnessed us giving multiple people a place to lay their head in temporary situations. We have had the opportunity to feed and minister to those in need. We focus on reaching out and helping people in whatever way we can and allowing our children to be a part of that. I make sure they value the opportunity to sow into someone else's life.

Sometimes we have fear that giving to someone will mean we don't have enough for ourselves. A true giver looks past their current needs and gives in spite of them.

We even practice this in our home. I love to see my children take time to give to each other and pick out just the right gift, or even make a gift for their siblings.

It is easy to be overtaken by selfishness when money gets tight. The number one way I break out of that cycle of selfishness is by giving. I try my best to help my children see and experience that freedom as well.

I remember when I took my eldest daughter to Zimbabwe. We had an amazing housekeeper that worked at our guest house. Gladys made a very long journey to work every day. One day we offered to take her home. It was a very humble mud home with a thatched roof. Her goal was to build herself a new brick home. Every paycheck Gladys would buy more bricks. She even offered to show us the home in it's building phase. I was so impressed with her fervor.

I had given my daughter spending money while we were there. She came to me one night and asked if she could give the housekeeper ten dollars to help her buy bricks for her new home. Ten dollars would buy Gladys fifty bricks. At first, I told her that she should keep her money and that I would give her something from both of us. Then I thought for a moment. Why would I deny her the opportunity to bless someone? Wasn't that the kind of heart I prayed my children would have? She was so proud to put money in a card to bless Gladys.

I am paid for what I do. However, most of what I do in other countries is pro bono. My desire is to see children removed from orphanages and cared for in local families. This takes precedence over financial gain. It is one way that my husband and I decided together that we would allow our family to be a blessing. The amazing result of happy families and healthy and safe children is priceless.

We encourage our children to give their time by serving in church as well. Our children love helping in the kitchen, ushering, working in media, youth ministry, and anywhere else they can be of assistance. This sets the stage for a giving heart that desires to be a blessing without any strings attached. We have also enjoyed serving together in local organizations that benefit our community.

My husband was an executive in a local organization that served the homeless, hungry, and offered recovery support for addictions. Our children were not able to be a part of this due to the nature of the organization.

However, my husband spent lots of time sharing stories, helping my children understand the plight of many of the people he worked with. He could have easily left work at work. Instead he instilled compassion and understanding in his children for people that many push aside. We are learning and growing together how to be givers.

> *"A true giver looks past their current needs and gives in spite of them."*

My oldest daughter has huge dreams to start an organization in Haiti. There is no doubt that much of her inspiration came from the exposure she has had witnessing poverty and need in other parts of the world. We encourage her drive to make her mark on this world, and continually fuel it with our own pursuits.

I love that children dream seemingly ridiculous dreams. When they are young, their thoughts about their future are limitless. What we may call "delusions of grandeur" are their innate desires to change the world. How can we keep that fire going? We help them by dreaming big and giving big ourselves. I pray that my children choose to always pour out their time, talent, and resources to bless the world in the areas of their greatest passions.

What do children learn when they watch their parents give?

- ❖ They learn that the world does not revolve around them.
- ❖ They become less self-focused.
- ❖ They learn how to use their time, talent, and money to be a blessing to others.
- ❖ They understand generosity and do not have to have a reason to give.

Dream Builder

- *Find a way to give your time.*

- *Find a way to give your talent.*

- *Find a way to give your resources.*

mom~spiration:
Give Together

Work together with your children to make someone else's day special.

mom~spiration #7

Let Them

See

Your Integrity

"Live so that when your children think of fairness, caring, and integrity, they think of you."
Unknown

Have you ever tried to teach a teenager something that you were not living yourself? Let's just say, they can smell a fraud from a mile away. You better believe they know when we are operating in integrity. They also know when we are just blowing smoke.

Our children need to see our integrity and upstanding character at home, on our jobs, in our ministries, and with complete strangers.

The way we go about handling sticky situations in front of them can make or break favor, partnerships, and ultimately our dreams. Our kids are watching.

I desperately want my children to see that lying, shortcuts, and undercutting others is not the way to the top. Even if it takes you longer to attain your goals, it is best to hold on to your integrity.

I've had to apologize in the past for not handling situations well. I've had to look my children in the face and admit my folly. It is not a good feeling. An even worse feeling is remaining in my pride and pretending that I was right.

> "You can never go wrong by doing what is right."
> Amber Lia

There have even been times when I have made promises I simply did not feel like keeping. When it was time to come through I stood at the crossroad between regret and humility. These are the moments that teach our children how to handle life, relationships, and business dealings.

One such moment I will never forget. My sixteen-year-old daughter is the author of four adventure books for kids. In the editing phase of the third book I added a few details to her book just before having the final copies printed. She expressed her anger so much so that it culminated into an intense argument that I am not proud of. I thought I knew what was best. However, it was not my place to change her story. I defended my position and pride until I came to the realization that this was not setting a good example. As an author myself, how would I feel if someone changed my body of work without consulting me? Even though I was taken aback when my integrity was called into question, I had to apologize and have the additions removed, and books reprinted.

"The way we go about handling sticky situations in front of them can make or break favor, partnerships and ultimately our dreams."

What we do in such moments teaches our kids how to operate in integrity, even when our pride wants to hang on to what we think is right. When they see us lie, gossip, take something, or even omit information in crucial situations, they are learning by our example.

When we pursue our dreams we must have standards of integrity that we are bound to, and we have to demonstrate that to our kids. In a world where business, Hollywood and the workplace can be shrewd, we must maintain our standards.

What do children learn by seeing our integrity?

- ❖ They learn that doing the right thing is always the right choice.
- ❖ They learn that real integrity shows when no one else is looking.
- ❖ They learn that you always win when you operate in integrity.

Dream Builder

Integrity is key to dream fulfillment. Make a list of things you will and/or will not do to maintain integrity as you pursue your dreams.

mom~spiration:
Talk About Integrity

Share with your kids about a time when you were tempted to do the wrong thing. Ask them the same thing. Discuss the importance of integrity and rewards of living a life with upstanding character. How can this affect your/their dreams?

mom~spiration #8

Let Them See You Make Mistakes

"Your dream doesn't have an expiration date. Take a deep breath, and try again."
Unknown

I remember the first time I said to my children, "I am human, just like you!" It was as if a light bulb had gone off in their heads. What? Mom makes mistakes too? Mom even screws things up sometimes. One thing I find myself saying often is, "I am sorry."

You are human. You make mistakes. There is no use in trying to hide your humanity from your children. They don't need a perfect mom. They need their real mom.

As you are pursuing your dreams there will be bumps in the road. Sometimes you will mess up big time as you are learning and growing your way to the top. Share those moments with your kids. Help them to see how you handle your own mistakes and fumbles.

They learn those things from you. You are teaching them to stand up and correct their path in the face of embarrassment, or to run the opposite direction in fear. Which lesson do you want to teach?

One of my greatest mistakes in every industry that I have worked, or dream I have pursued, was undervaluing myself. I never gave myself enough credit for being the expert that I was, or for having what it took to do well at what I was pursuing. You better believe that our children pick up on our self-doubt.

In the beginning of my speaking career I received counsel from a few mentors that suggested what I should be charging for my training, keynotes, and consultations. I was so eager to accept every invitation that I did not listen to the counsel that was given to me.

After a while, I found myself in a rut with a group of non-profits that all communicated amongst themselves the rates that I gave them; which were very low. I was in a situation where I could not increase my rates for fear of losing opportunities. This was a steep learning curve. I have since valued and stuck to what I know my wisdom, expertise, and services are worth. I had to correct that mistake.

I found my daughter feeling down about the sales of her books. I shared my epic fail and how it affected my progress. I had to share with her that others only value your service or product if you value it. It is important to represent yourself and your offerings as significant and worthy of someone else's investment. Through sharing this mistake and encouraging her, she has begun to represent herself as a talented and skillful author, and not just a kid who wrote a few books.

> *"Help them to see how you handle your own mistakes and fumbles."*

This same mistake that I made in devaluing my gift helped me give my oldest son perspective on himself. This child is an extremely intellectual and bright young man. His dad and I began to notice that he was not sharing his knowledge and experience as a science and aviation expert around other teens. He felt like no one wanted to hear what he had to say.

We were seeing yet the same mistake take shape of not valuing who you are and what you have to offer the world. I knew the signs and I needed to encourage him to share who he is and what he knows with the world. He learned how to find the right crowd that wants to appreciate who he is. Now he can bounce his knowledge and ideas off people of like minds.

This skill is crucial. The mistake of holding back your greatness can have lasting impact on your dreams and your kids. I had to teach my children that others value what you have to offer when YOU value yourself.

It is important that we use our folly and mistakes to help give our kids perspective and keep them from making the same mistakes as they pursue their dreams.

What do children learn when they see us make mistakes?

- ❖ They see us as human beings instead of perfection.
- ❖ They understand that there are always do-overs and second chances.
- ❖ They learn how to laugh at themselves and not hide in shame or embarrassment.

Dream Builder

Is there a mistake that you have made in your career or passionate pursuits? How can you correct that mistake? How can you make sure that it does not repeat itself as you move forward toward new dreams?

mom~spiration:
Share Your Mistakes

Share a time with your kids that you made a silly mistake. Share another time when you made a big mistake and how you recovered. Ask them about mistakes they have made. Discuss do-overs and grace.

mom~spiration #9

Let Them See You Break Barriers

"The only place where your dream becomes impossible is in your own thinking."
Robert H. Schuller

*W*e all have barriers to our dreams. ==Many of them are invisible barriers we create in our mind.== Others can be placed upon us by people or society at large.

What are your barriers? Some barriers are perceived and others are very real. Could it be that you are a woman trying to enter a male dominated field? A minority entering a majority field? Is your barrier confidence, education, or finances? Do you have physical limitations? Mental illness? Whatever they are, we owe it to ourselves and our children to kick down those barriers and pursue what makes our heart happy! God can knock those limitations down fast if we trust Him to do it.

How about the fact that you are "simply" a mom? Sometimes we think our dreams are limited due to the responsibility of our family. Whatever those barriers are, there is a way over, around, under, or even through them.

There are barriers that are external such as relational, cultural, political, geographical, educational, and financial.

Before I journeyed across the waters to conduct a training for social workers in Ethiopia and Ghana, I was very nervous. I was afraid that I would say or do something that would be improper in their eyes. The cultural barriers stopped me in my tracks on many occasions. I learned so much through being brave and stepping out of my comfort zone anyway.

That first experience gave me the confidence to pretty much go anywhere in the world and move fluidly through their customs and traditions with ease. Whether it is ministering to a mom on the floor of a mud hut, touring a marble palace in the Middle East, or spending the day with a group of people that speak an entirely different language - I can laugh, cry, and share all the things we have in common. I feel at home wherever I am in the world. I want my children to feel the same way.

Part of our family's vision is to travel the world. My husband and I focus a lot of effort in sharing our cultural experiences across multiple continents with our children to prepare them for a global life. We do this by travel, reading, and exposing them to a variety of cultural experiences. This helps kick down stigmas, prejudices, opinions, and judgments that can be barriers to their dreams.

Then there are very personal barriers such as learning challenges, physical disabilities, and mental illness. These barriers can be even more difficult to overcome.

> "The things that make us different can be the things that make us strong."
> Nathan Clarkson

I am so blessed to have had a mother who defied many odds. In particular, mental illness. She struggled with manic depression and paranoia. Through all of her difficulties and pitfalls, she plowed toward a better life for us.

She did not let her mental illness keep her from working and perfecting her skills. She did not allow it to stop her from eventually buying her dream home, graduating college, volunteering, and being a blessing to people around her. She broke barriers. That taught me volumes about barriers; they are temporary and always conquerable.

I appreciate my mom's encouragement. During my childhood and into college, I was severely terrified of math. I had a lack of confidence and diminished my dreams as a result. It seemed insurmountable and impossible to understand basic math. I felt as if it would affect my future greatly. I never did become a math whiz, but I have become confident in God's calling, gifts, and direction for my life. I know what I need to know to accomplish His purpose for me.

> *"Some barriers are perceived and others are very real."*

Interestingly enough, I have several children that have learning challenges. My own struggle has given me the unique perspective to encourage their natural gifting. I will pull out all the stops to knock down those barriers.

We continually seek out alternative ways of learning math to conquer dyscalculia. We have also utilized out-of-the-box methods to help our child with dyslexia. Another child with dysgraphia has gained confidence in communicating his brilliance to the world through voice-to-text software, dictation, and typing. We only see barriers as detours, not the end of the road.

I help them to see that God has equipped them for their dreams by highlighting their talents and giving them opportunity to showcase who they really are. Doing this helps them remain inspired to conquer their barriers, and to accomplish what God placed in their heart.

Take the focus off you and your children's barriers. Put the focus on individual gifting and abilities that will encourage them to move forward.

What do our children learn from watching us break barriers?

- They learn that barriers can be broken.
- They see that some barriers are invisible and only in our mind.
- They are likely to break them as well when seeing us do this.
- They have a broader and more positive perspective on what is possible for themselves.

Dream Builder

Are there current barriers to your dreams in your mind, body, finances, relationships, or career? What can you do today to push past them?

mom~spiration:
Break Barriers Together

Share with your kids the barriers to your past, career, or dreams that you have overcome. How did you overcome them? Ask your children about the barriers they may feel need to be broken for them to accomplish their dreams.

mom~spiration #10
Let Them See You Juggle Fire

"Never give up on a dream just because of the time it will take... The time will pass anyway."
Earl Nightingale

*H*ave you ever watched a clown juggle and thought, "Let me try that"? Have you ever picked up the same number of balls and attempted to do the same thing only to make a complete fool of yourself? Sometimes we see someone juggling an impossible amount of responsibilities, and we come down on ourselves for not being able to do the same thing.

It is important to note that each of us have grace for the responsibilities and roles we have to juggle at each stage of our lives. It is impossible for me to juggle yours, and you don't have the grace to juggle mine.

Marriage, children, household obligations, jobs, college, church, community organizations, extended family commitments, businesses, financial obligations, and the list goes on. There are so many things that we have to keep up with.

When our children observe us juggling and maintaining balance within all of our current areas of grace, they learn a lot. It shows them that it can be done.

> "If you get tired, learn to rest, not quit."
> Banksy

Juggling multiple responsibilities takes practice and skill. I learned something very early in my mom journey. I may not be able to juggle it all every single day. However, I can determine what is important today, tomorrow, and next week. In other words, each day is going to have its own list of priorities.

==You know you are juggling well when your family's needs are taken care of physically, emotionally, and spiritually.== As a mom I can feel when things are not aligned. I can feel distanced from my husband due to the busyness of life. I notice when my children are distant and struggling. These are RED FLAGS for me. Based on those two factors, I determine if adding or removing a new venture to my plate is the right thing to do.

You will also know if you are juggling well if your business, clients, and other people that depend on you are being handled with excellence. If you find that the struggle between family and your goals are clashing, it is time for an evaluation or shift in how you manage your life.

I have not always been good at juggling multiple things. Due to my propensity for extreme tunnel vision, it was common for me to drop balls all over the place. If I was working on a project, or started a new venture, it consumed me day and night. Anything in the way was pushed aside. After becoming a mother, this was problematic. It took some time for me to adjust to the idea that I had to juggle more than one important thing. I learned to prioritize daily who and what needed my full attention.

How well we handle our responsibilities shows in our frustration levels and ability to give our attention to what is most important at the moment. Our children learn by watching this and observing our willingness to put them at the top of our list, after dad of course.

In preparation for an international conference or during an intense season of writing, I am tunnel focused. I have to intentionally set aside one-on-one time with each of my children. This shows my family that their needs are important to me during busy seasons.

"You know you are juggling well if your family's needs are taken care of physically, emotionally, and spiritually."

When you are busy, pause and check in with your family. Be sure that they are getting what they need during those busy seasons of dream fulfillment.

What do our children learn from seeing us juggle fire?

- They learn how to multi-task.
- They learn that pursuing dreams takes drive and energy.
- They learn how to prioritize what is important.

Dream Builder

Write down all the roles and responsibilities you have. Then indicate which roles and responsibilities are high priority. Decide whether the others are necessary or if they are distractions to your progress.

mom~spiration:
Juggle Fire

Make a plan with your kids to "juggle fire" together. Discuss how you can make things easier for each other to pursue your dreams.

mom~spiration #11

Let Them See

You Invest

"Devote yourself to the idea. Go make it happen. Struggle on it. Overcome your fears, smile. Don't forget: this is your dream."

Unknown

*Y*ou have heard the saying, "It takes money to make money." You have also heard that, "You get what you pay for." They both give the message that investment is key to success.

Yes, this is true with financial and business transactions. However, it is also true when it comes to investing your time and effort into your dreams.

Invest your TIME. The more time you spend perfecting your craft, the better you will be. This is a consistent conversation I have with my children. Anything worth pursuing takes time and effort, even when it is hard.

Invest Your TALENT. Dig deep and pull out all those skills and talents that have been hidden away for way too long. Use every gift you have to bring your dreams closer to reality. Don't hold back. Teach your children how to do the same by highlighting what they do well.

Invest Your RESOURCES. We value the things we invest our money in. We tend to hold it near and dear to our hearts when our hard earn dollars are put toward something. Give yourself a budget and use it wisely. Any dream worth pursuing will need a financial investment to accomplish. Don't be overwhelmed by this. Sometimes it is as simple as hiring a consultant, designer, legal counsel, or just paying for a monthly website to get started.

Dreams don't come easy. No one is going to manufacture your dream, or pull your dream out of a lottery and hand it to you. It takes an investment of your time, talent, resources, and determination to make it happen.

What kind of investment are you making in your dreams? Do your children witness the investments that you make on a regular basis?

As a mom, I make it a priority to invest in things that will inspire my kid's dreams. If there is a class, an event, conference, book, activity, or subscription that will give them direction and information for their goals, then I am all in.

I am learning to do this for myself. Sometimes we will invest all kinds of time and money into our kid's dream fulfillment, but we don't look at our own dreams as seriously.

I remember finding a course for one of my children that was very costly. It would allow him to take his animation skills to another level. I also remember investing a hefty chunk of money in a camp for another child that would take her dream of becoming a film maker to another level. It took me no time at all to pay and invest in their dreams. When it came time for me to invest in classes, conferences, or travel to enhance my own skills and passion, I second guessed myself. Why?

I always felt guilty for investing in myself. Buying myself clothes, getting a gym membership, paying for a class, or any number of things I desired, never made the budget. The kids needed clothes, shoes, music lessons, uniforms, sports equipment, and fun activities. There was never room for my frivolous mom desires.

The truth is, the more I invest in myself, at the nudge of my husband, the better mom I become. It is not selfish to take care of yourself and to invest in the things you need. You even need to give yourself permission to invest in things you want from time to time.

I challenge you to find ways to invest in the future of your dreams in multiple ways. Give yourself permission to spend the money and the time to become well versed and prepared for the next level of your passionate pursuit.

Invest in your image. Make an investment in the things that will give you the confidence to stand out in a crowd in your field. You will feel better, look better, and have the boldness to approach new things when you like what you see in the mirror.

Invest in your knowledge. What bodies of knowledge do you need to master to become an expert in your field? What kind of opportunities are available in your region that will allow you to grow and learn in this area? Local classes, library programs, community colleges, technical trade schools, or even local professionals that will allow you to shadow; all of these options could give you a great start toward your goals.

"Sometimes we will invest all kinds of time and money into our kid's dream fulfillment, but we don't look at our own dreams as seriously."

Invest in your technology. This does not have to be expensive. Think about the technology you need for designing, blogging, recording, or even writing. Find the best products, apps, software, and computers your money can buy. The way you present yourself on-line is important. The right technology can make all the difference.

All of these areas of investment will take your connections and your dreams to a new level. Do not be afraid to put money and effort into the things you want to accomplish.

What do children learn from watching us invest in our dreams?

- ❖ They see that dreams don't just happen on their own.
- ❖ They witness what it takes to achieve their goals.
- ❖ They learn to invest in themselves and their growth.
- ❖ They learn that investing in yourself is not selfish, but self-love.

Dream Builder

What investments do you need to make to take your dream to the next level? Research opportunities to invest and pour more into your vision.

mom~spiration:
Invest Time, Talent & Resources

Come up with ideas that you can invest time, talent, and resources in each other's dreams. How can you help your children reach their goals? How can they help you reach yours?

mom~spiration #12

Let Them See You Sweat

"If your dreams don't scare you they are not big enough."
Unknown

*D*reaming is the easy part. It is in the doing that things get messy and unpredictable. The sweaty, scary roads toward our dreams are the ones we don't talk much about.

We tend to envy a person's final display of victory. What they have not shared with you is the hard work and excruciating life changes they endured in order to make it happen.

Sometimes there are years between the dream and the fruition of said dream. All of the stuff in between is where the real exhilaration is.

Have you ever had a goal that was reached that took everything you had in you to accomplish? The victory was much sweeter once you completed it based on the effort and drive it took to reach your destination.

Our kids need to see all the messiness in between. Let them in on all the work and mountains that you had to climb along the way. Share the lessons learned and the work ethic involved in accomplishing your goals, both big and small.

I use to struggle with the "doing" part. I had all kinds of goal lists, mission statements, dream journals, confessions, and vision boards. I would look at them and dream of the distant future when my life would resemble all the pictures I had collected. However, I wasn't taking action. I am reminded often of God's word that says,

"...faith without works is dead". It wasn't until I started moving my feet and activating my faith that God met me right where I was. I started doing something and He started moving mountains and making connections on my behalf. You have to act, even if it is one step at a time.

> "There are only two days in the year that nothing can be done. One is yesterday and the other is tomorrow, so today is the right day to love, believe, do, and mostly live."
> Dalai Lama

Working hard and working smart are two different things. As moms with a lot on our plate, ==we have to make sure effort is being put into the right things.== We want to see progress and not go in circles while wearing ourselves out – then calling it work.

There was a deodorant commercial when I was growing up. Their slogan was "Never let them see you sweat." When it comes to your children, they need to see you sweat. They need to watch the process, progress, and making of a dream.

Step by step my children have watched me work, fumble, try again, and accomplish each stage of my dream. I am home full time with them as we homeschool. Our days are a mix of learning, growing, and pursuing both their dreams and my own. I cannot hide away in a cocoon and emerge victorious. I am living, learning, growing, and working hard right beside them.

One of my dreams was to be an author. For many years I dismissed the possibility when multiple people suggested that I write a book. I had so many interests and passions, I had no idea what to write about.

When the season came, the grace was there. I certainly had no idea that my first book would be about homeschooling. I worked very hard to create a piece of work I could be proud of that my readers could connect with. "Homeschool Gone Wild" has done very well and the reviews have brought tears to my eyes. When you have labored over a project for a period of time and have shed blood and tears to make it great, the reward is magnificent. My children were there to see it all.

"Sometimes there are years between the dream and the fruition of said dream. All of the stuff in between is where the real exhilaration is."

My oldest son is a pilot in training. I am constantly getting unsolicited praise for his work ethic, breadth of knowledge, and passion for aviation and engineering. It comes from family, friends, random people he meets, and his flight school instructors. I could say that it is just the way he is made up, but that is not entirely true. I firmly believe that part of it is his observation of the things we share with him and in front of him about our own journey toward our dreams. He has an example he can touch.

I have watched my youngest daughter take on a passion for sewing and creating amazing things. She has created countless prototypes of her technical and sewing projects. Her first draft or project is never the last. She will work until she gets it perfectly, because it is her goal to sell her products one day. This tenacity comes from within her. It also comes from watching us challenge ourselves to try harder, do better, and continually perfect our craft.

The sweat that you put into perfecting what you do or offer is not always physical work. Sometimes it is more time, brain power, or making the right connections to take your dream to the next level. Your kids learn from watching and being a part of this process.

What do our children learn by watching us work hard for our dreams?

- ❖ They learn the difference between working hard and working smart.
- ❖ They learn lessons in work ethic and tenacity.
- ❖ They enjoy the fruits of their hard work.

Dream Builder

What areas require you to put in more work, effort, time, and elbow grease? How can you rearrange your daily priorities to have a more intense focus on your dreams?

mom~spiration:
Work Hard Together

What challenging goal can you work together to achieve with your children? How can you use each of yourself and your children's strengths to pursue a family goal?

mom~spiration #13

Let Them See Order

"The difference between a dream and a goal is a deadline."
Unknown

*O*ne of our earlier mom~spirations focused on juggling fire and multiple responsibilities. Doing this is very difficult without order. It takes organization and the right systems in place in order to juggle motherhood, work, business, and everything else on your plate.

I am sure you would agree that when we are scattered and in a frenzy our kids tend to follow suit. Developing order and peace in our homes as well as in our pursuits brings a sense of stability.

Our kids learn so much when we involve them in the planning and organizing of our lives. Even more so when they are able to see how we accomplish our dreams and goals; it helps them to see how order establishes clear thoughts, concrete direction, and the value of time.

My oldest daughter is an author. We share a love for words and books. I spent almost 20 years as a ghost writer and editor. Those skills gave me the systems and planning strategies to help her organize her book projects in a way that help her work fluidly and efficiently.

On any given day we are each working on writing projects and are able to bounce ideas off of each other with titles, content, design, and other details. It is a shared dream and a connection that is deeply valued. It is my hope to be a continual inspiration as she paves her way into the literary and film writing world.

"Anything that costs you your peace is too expensive."
Unknown

Managing your time wisely spills over into your family. ==We are less likely to achieve our goals if we don't value our time and how we use it.== This is a gift you can give to your children.

The way we focus on learning in our home gives my children the opportunity to manage their own time, projects, and important tasks.

As a family, our individual time is intertwined with one another. We learn how to give each other the grace and space to create, write, do projects, and attend events by managing our time together. If we give our children a chance, they are much more capable of handling themselves and their tasks than we give them credit for.

At the beginning of every year, we meet with each of our children and find out what their current goals are for themselves. What would they like to learn, master, or achieve that year? Then we hunt for opportunities to help them reach those goals. It is up to them to manage their time and resources to achieve those goals with our sideline coaching. This will benefit our kids in their future endeavors. When entering college or the work force, they will not be in shock when they suddenly have to manage their time and efficiency on their own. They will have already mastered the skill.

"Managing your time wisely spills over into your family."

==Another key to order is simplicity and decluttering your life.== I have always been one to keep an orderly and tidy home. When I became a mom of six children and suddenly had to manage a household of eight people, it became increasingly difficult to maintain; with three of them being borderline hoarders. Managing a family of eight means managing all the stuff that comes with eight people.

Recently, I began addressing my obsession with collecting things, in particular, books and learning resources for my children. Most of it went unused and just took up space.

We spent a few weeks discussing the importance of simplicity and peace. Room by room we simplified and got rid of everything that was unnecessary and taking up space; clothes, shoes, toys, and books. As my husband drove away to the donation site, a weight was lifted. I felt lighter and able to breathe.

> "Simplicity is the ultimate form of sophistication."
> Leonardo da Vinci

Ridding ourselves of all the extra stuff allows us to make room for clear thoughts, meaningful things, and space. Believe it or not at the end of this process, my children and husband began getting rid of things and changing their perspective on decluttering their own lives. So much so, one of my children that was an extreme collector of things, has created a goal to become a minimalist. This is major progress and we all benefit from it.

Things clutter our world and take precious time and space from the things that can benefit our dreams and goals. When we declutter our lives, we declutter our minds. That gives way to creativity, innovative ideas, and inspiration.

What do children learn from witnessing order and clear vision?

- ❖ They learn that having a vision and plan is the best way to start a pursuit.
- ❖ They learn that a plan will keep them focused during distracting seasons in life.
- ❖ They learn that they are in charge of their plan; they can change it at any moment.

Dream Builder

Disorder can steal our dreams. Is there a part of your life that requires an organizational overhaul? Make a plan to rid yourself of all the time and dream-stealers.

mom~spiration:
Organize & Plan Together

Come up with a plan to accomplish a family task, vacation, or community event with your children. Involve them in the vision, organization and execution of the plan.

mom~spiration #14
Let Them See You Fight

"Fight for your dreams, and your dreams will fight for you."
Paulo Coelho
The Alchemist

Are you a fighter? Not a physical fighter, but do you fight? Life can kick at us sometimes. When we are pursuing things that seem impossible or all the odds are stacked against us, we have to know how to fight.

I come from a long line of women who were fighters on both sides of my family. The circumstances they overcame and the hurdles they had to jump in life seemed insurmountable. They did it! I truly learned from the best.

In 2014, I traveled to Ethiopia. I had the pleasure of meeting an amazing woman. She was the ultimate fighter. I will call her Hannah and I would like to share her story with you.

Hannah was the mother of six children. Being a mother of six myself, we instantly connected. She was faced with placing her children in an orphanage. Hannah had recently been widowed and her husband was the breadwinner of her family. There was no possible way that she could provide for her children and her mother. In her country, mothers face this impossible circumstance every single day.

Just imagine having to face giving up your children for no other reason than you cannot feed or provide for them. What a heart wrenching choice to have to make.

Hannah committed to a program that would help her start her own business in an effort to give her income and in turn keep her children. I have never seen a woman fight so hard to succeed for the sake of her kids.

As a result of that program, she learned how to start a business and market herself. While I was there, she invited myself and the team to her home. She performed a traditional coffee ceremony and shared with us how much her life changed simply by deciding to fight, learn something new, and work hard.

Not only did Hannah start a business. She started several businesses. She began walking children to school for working parents who could not do so. She began renting out her courtyard for the neighbor's donkey and goats. She began selling eggs, produce, and goats milk at the market. She even rented out a small space in her modest mud and brick home to a boarder. Her businesses may seem unconventional to us, but they kept her family together. They also paid for her children's school fees, books, and uniforms.

Imagine what her children learned from watching her fight. She accomplished a dream of becoming an entrepreneur and was able to keep her children out of the orphanage. Can you imagine the life lessons they experienced and dreams they will dream as a result of their mother's example? She fought by using her talents, current resources, and hard work while saving her family in the process.

We have to fight! Fight for our families, our dreams, and our children's dreams. When our kids see us fight it will strengthen their resolve to fight and to stick with things until they see results, even when they are hard.

"Can you imagine the life lessons they experienced and dreams they will dream as a result of their mother's example?"

Sometimes we have to be willing to take risks to see our dreams manifest. Your dream may require a skill you have never operated in before. Will you let that stop you? You may say, "I hate my job but I need to work to provide for my family. I have dreams, but who has time for that?"

One thing is for sure – time will pass whether you pursue your dreams or not. Why not go for it? Why not fight for the passion that lies within your heart? Your dream may involve major profits from selling a product or service. Every dream has a different measurement of success. My dream involves the non-profit sector.

My kids have had to watch me fight for my dream over the last handful of years. Although I do a lot of work in the United States, most of my work is done in other countries. I am paid for all the work that I do in the US. However, the countries that ask me to come conduct training for families cannot afford to pay all of my costs. In situations like these you must know what God is instructing you to do. When you know you are on the right track, you are willing to fight for your dream.

After several years of travel and fighting to either fund my travel myself or appeal to investors to support my work as a small organization, I became extremely discouraged. I questioned whether I had come to the end of my work. I went to Thailand for a global children's advocate summit. I wondered if it was my last international trip.

The last day of the Summit was a surprise. Instead of having more speakers and program presentations, it was set-up for prayer and impartation for all of the advocates to get refueled and encouraged. I spent the entire morning praying and asking God for direction for the future of my organization. Even though we were small with few investors, we had done impactful work around the world and I was not ready to give up.

That morning God showed me a picture of a map with lines scribbled all across it signifying the global reach of iSpeak4KidsGlobal. I asked God that day, how we would get funding for that. His words, "YOU PAY FOR IT!"

Whoa! What? Here I am looking for an answer to our funding problem and He is telling me to pay for it myself. When I returned home, I shared the map I saw with my husband. I told him what God said; pay for it ourselves. My husband's response, "If God told us to fund this work, then He must have a plan to provide what we need to do it."

My kids were able to see all of this in progress. They saw the investment we were making in the lives of children across the world and how hard we were working to obtain funding.

Several trips took place after that year. Many family's lives were impacted as a result of our willingness to fight for what we knew was right. There was still a feeling of defeat as we struggled to continue our work.

A few years later, my husband and I had dinner with great friends. We sat at dinner encouraging each other towards our dreams. We brainstormed ideas to help one another. My dear friend said, "You have so much knowledge and experience in foster care, adoption, and homeschooling, you should write books on the topics. The books can fund your work."

Light bulbs went off! I had been told for years that I needed to write. I always shrugged it off as something to do later in life. Hearing her say this on that day, it felt right. Now was the time and this was my answer. I began writing a month later, and published my first book five months later. That book immediately yielded funds that supported my work. Here you are reading my second book!

Our kids saw us fight and work hard to accomplish this dream. They learned that nothing is out of reach if you press in and fight for it.

I am willing to go wherever I feel God is sending me. He has always come through and made a way for us to fund every trip. I will speak to a conference hall full of people in the US. I will train under a tent in the middle of a farm in Malawi - in the rain to people who are willing to open their modest homes to children without families. I will sit on the floor of a mud hut in Ethiopia and console a foster mom who needs encouragement. I am willing to work hard by providing quality books on my end that in turn bring them this service. The smiles on a child's face and the open hearts of the foster and adoptive parents make it all worth it.

If you are reading this book or any of my other books, you can be proud to have supported our work. Every book you purchase published by iS4Kids Publishing goes toward training foster parents across the globe. This is an effort to remove children from institutions and place them in loving families right in their own communities. Every child deserves a loving home.

What do children learn from seeing us fight?

- ❖ They learn that their dreams are worth fighting for.
- ❖ They learn not to accept defeat so easily.
- ❖ They learn to fight smart.

Dream Builder

Dreams don't always come easy. What do you believe will be the greatest fight you have to engage in order to reach your dream? How will you fight? What are your weapons and strategies to win?

mom~spiration:
Conquer Something Together

Everyone identify a personal or professional struggle worth conquering (job, school, weight, dream, skill, etc.). Together encourage, pray, and help each other conquer the struggles you identify.

mom~spiration #15
Let Them See You Stand For Something

"I alone cannot change the world, but I can cast a stone across the waters to create many ripples."
Mother Teresa

Our convictions make us who we are. The causes we stand for and the issues we defend are near and dear to our hearts.

When we share our passions and the things we hold dear with our kids, they see more of who we are. They also see us stand up for the things that are just. They get a front row seat to watch us defend those that need defending and protect those that need protection.

What do you stand for? Have you brought your children along into those spaces of advocacy? Do your children understand why you feel the way you feel and the reasons behind your passion for such a cause?

There are a lot of areas my husband and I are passionate about. However, the biggest space of advocacy for us is foster care and adoption. Of course, having adopted all of our children, this is near and dear to our hearts.

Most importantly, we stand for every child that needs a family and a home. An institution is not a place for a child to grow up. Secondly, families need to be trauma competent and properly equipped to nurture and compassionately parent traumatized children.

My kids watch my tenacity and passion in this area and have taken on much of the same train of thought. It does not stop there. We don't require our children to take on our causes or passions.

They support it and cheer us on as we stand for the 152 million orphans and foster children globally. However, what they learn from watching is so much more. They learn to stand up for something they believe in. They learn how to advocate for someone or something that is on their heart.

How valuable a lesson this is. They learn very early that their voice matters and they have the power to do something about injustices in the world. This is huge!

One of my sons keeps a running list of all the things he is going to change when he becomes President. Will he become President? I don't know. What I do know is that he is confident in his ability to change his corner of the world for good.

I have a daughter who is passionate about sustainable missions. She desires to help women earn income to take care of their families in order to keep their children out of orphanages or off the street. She is interested in educating and inspiring people to be their best.

My oldest son, the pilot in training, has mentioned piloting charter planes that fly high risk missions. The missions provide medical care and emergency supplies in remote and hard to reach places all over the world. This is his desire in addition to a multitude of other things he wants to do in the aviation industry.

"They learn very early that their voice matters and they have the power to do something about injustices in the world."

All of our children's passion came from seeing our passion to stand for something. Exposure to a variety of experiences, places, people, and causes will spark passion in your children. Exposure will ignite the fire on the inside of them!

What do our children learn by watching us STAND up for what we are passionate about?

- ❖ They learn that their voice is important.
- ❖ They learn that one person can make a difference.
- ❖ They learn to recognize and call out injustice.
- ❖ They learn to care and support the needs of others.

Dream Builder

What cause is related to your passion? How can you make a difference in that industry or arena by expressing that passion?

mom~spiration:
Stand for Something Together

Involve your children in a cause that is near and dear to your heart. Do research together. Join a local group that will allow you to make an impact side by side.

mom~spiration #16

Let Them See You Win

"I don't dream at night, I dream for a living."
Steven Spielberg

*M*y husband experienced an upset in his career in executive leadership about five years ago. He never stopped pressing, believing, working, and connecting with new opportunities. Of course he worked the entire time, but it was not what he ultimately wanted to do. This past year, he connected and began to serve with an organization. Within the year, he was unanimously voted in as the President of the Board of Directors. His passion for the cause and his tenacity to stay the course sustained him until the opportunity arose for him to serve in ways he always desired. Five years passed between the opportunities, but he never gave up.

Our kids had a front row seat to see dad win and achieve a longstanding goal. It was cause for celebration! Every single milestone and step toward your dream is worthy of celebration. Include your children in that celebration.

Since I began traveling and speaking globally, I have never promoted or marketed myself. It is important to me to offer quality inspiration and information everywhere that I go. As word spread about my work, opportunities arose.

My kids had a chance to sit back and watch God do His thing as we walked through all the right doors. Each step, each opportunity, we celebrate our wins; big or small.

This reminds me of the planning stages of my book launch party for "Homeschool Gone Wild". I had originally planned on having the party for adults only.

Meaning my children would not be there, nor would anyone else's. It sounded like a great idea at the time, after all, it was my party to celebrate my accomplishment, right?

> *"Every single milestone and step toward your dream is worthy of celebration."*

I began to think about the fact that my children were just as excited about this accomplishment as I was. They inspired the book in the first place. Why wouldn't I have them present at one of the most exciting days of my life?

Having my kids there was amazing. They got to see me fight, struggle, lose sleep, work hard, and ultimately reach my goal. They were there to see it all and it was a beautiful experience to have them involved in the celebration that day.

Our kids need to see us win! Why? They need to see winning is possible. After watching all the work it takes to accomplish a goal, they get to witness the victory. What better learning opportunity can they have than that?

> "Sometimes life is about risking everything for a dream no one can see but you."
> -unknown

Winning is a process. Every step you successfully take toward your dreams is a win. Never feel like you have to be at the peak of the mountain to celebrate. That peak is ever-changing and the dream increases with every growth opportunity.

Giving up on our dreams does not benefit us or our children. Our kids are relying on us to show them how to approach life without limitations. There are many times I wanted to give up on my dream. Things became really hard dealing with funding limitations, visa issues, in-country dangers, language and cultural barriers, as well as the mom guilt of leaving my kids each time. I had to push pass them to win. I had to press on in order to see God do His thing in and through me. I am so far from where I want to be and what I want to accomplish. Giving up is not an option. Pause, catch your breath, rest for a moment if you must, but DO NOT STOP. Your kids are watching!

Working toward a win involves lots of stumbling and course correction. There will be a lot of struggles and moments when you wonder if you will win at all. Witnessing all of the ups and downs teaches our children to stick things out and work things through until they see the prize in sight.

As you set an example - dream, have fun, organize, sweat, give, exercise your faith, operate in integrity, and push towards your dreams. Take your kids on the ride of a lifetime with you.

Do you remember the Proverbs 31 woman we explored in the beginning of this book? All my life I focused on all of her spiritual and domestic virtues. Not once did I explore her ingenuity or her entrepreneurial spirit. It never occurred to me that she was a woman skillful at juggling diverse tasks. She accomplished what so many of us long to do as wives, mothers, business women, and career women. This woman made it happen and shows us that we can too!

God really does desire for us to accomplish His design for our lives. I pray you see that you don't have to sacrifice the well-being of your marriage or your children for a dream.

What an amazing ride your children will experience to see, touch, and witness victory with you. The lessons learned along the way will be priceless and empowering toward their very own dreams.

What do our children learn from watching us win?

- ❖ They learn to stay the course no matter how long it takes.
- ❖ They learn how to recognize big and small reasons to celebrate.
- ❖ They know how to give themselves credit for a job well done.
- ❖ They learn enough about themselves to develop habits that lead to their next win.

Dream Builder

Acknowledge your WINS! Give yourself credit for each phase completed, big or small. Plan something just for yourself to celebrate your WIN!

mom~spiration:
Win Together

Plan a "we win" party for the family. Celebrate something that each person in the family has worked hard at and congratulate them.

mom~spiration #17

Re-Discover Your mom~spiration

"She remembered who she was and the game changed."
Lalah Deliah

I am sure there were plenty of ah-ha moments as you read this book. I pray you were inspired to do something about your dreams and go big.

This is a call to action! I am challenging you to answer these questions honestly and completely. Answer them based on your heart's desire and what you believe God has put on the inside of you. Do not answer based on others' plans and ideas for what you should be doing with your life.

Take some time alone to sit and ponder. Pray and consider your true heart's desire. You may be surprised at your own answers.

What were your childhood dreams?

What dreams kept creeping into your heart as you read this book?

List 4-5 gifts/talents you have always been praised for.

When is the last time you operated in those gifts/talents? Did you maximize them?

What do you need to do to re-ignite those talents, gifts, or hobbies?

What group of people or industry do you feel drawn to?

What types of injustices or problems do you desire to solve?

What can you do today to begin a journey toward those dreams?

How can you involve your children as you work toward those dreams?

What do you believe God has called you to do? What impact are you determined to make in your lifetime?

Where will you go from here? Write your mom~spiration Vision Statement.

mom~spiration #18

Discover Your Children's Gifts & Dreams

"The goal of parenting shouldn't be to prepare children to withstand the world, but to grow children who will change the world."
L.R. Knost

*E*very day our children give us clues. The questions they ask. The things they love. The choices they make. The people, places, and things that bring them joy. They are all clues if we pay close enough attention. In my book, "Homeschool Gone WILD", I talk about paying close attention to your child's natural bent.

The following questions will help you focus in on who your child actually is. I encourage you to lay aside their struggles and challenges. Pay attention only to what they love and what they choose to do when given the freedom to explore. It may require you to observe your children over a few weeks to really pick up on their clues.

What have been my child's consistent interests over time?

How frequently and in what ways do they engage in the above interests?

What does my child choose to do when left completely alone?

What do they enjoy the most about what they are choosing to do?

What gifts and talents do they exhibit that stand out?

What opportunities can I give them to shine bright?

How can I encourage and inspire them in this area?

What are the dreams that your child has expressed?

Do your research! List all of the books, activities, classes, community programs, field trips, and mentors that can help your child get closer to their dream.

Epilogue

"Dreams come a size too big so we can grow into them."
-unknown

I am not the same person I was before I stepped out to pursue my dreams. I can truly say that I am a different mom. I see things differently. I recognize the power that I have in influencing my children, their dreams, and their confidence in God's call on their lives by living boldly and joyfully in my own purpose.

My greatest dream is to travel the globe with my husband and all of my children together. We have seen glimpses of this dream come true in trips that we have been able to take with a few of our kids individually to other countries. This is a dream I will continue to work toward.

"Dream openly, boldly, and courageously in front of your children."

Every step I take and venture I pursue, I am constantly trying to expose them to each moment. Every experience, hurdle, victory, and blooper along the way enriches their experience and gives them a perspective many children never get to see.

Get excited about who you are. Get excited about who your children are called to be. Together, as a family, blaze a trail straight toward the things that have been dormant on the inside of you for way too long.

To learn more about igniting the passion and interests of your children, read my first book "Homeschool Gone Wild', which is for ALL parents who are interested in highlighting the unique gifts and talents of their children.

I encourage you to step out. Pursue the things you have put on the back burner. Include your entire family in that pursuit and encourage one another toward destiny. Let them see, experience, and learn from the pursuit of your greatest passions.

Karla Marie Williams

Acknowledgements

I would like to acknowledge my dear husband whose support and grace allows me to be my best self. Thank you for being flexible and patient with me as I write and create bodies of work I can be proud of. You are the real MVP.

Thank you to my children for your continual support of mommy's ventures. I pray you will be inspired to be all that God has called you to be.

Finally, I would like to thank my sister, Nicole Spencer for being my long time editor, objective reader, and cheerleader. Also, my dear friends Lisa Faber, Lynn Pfund, Regina Traylor, Meghan Killeen, and Tira Hunter, my beta-readers. They have supported me with their kind words, prayers, and feedback to help make this book an impactful work of art.

Connect with Karla

Facebook
Unschooling the Sensational Six

Instagram
Unschooling the Sensational 6

YouTube
Unschooling the Sensational Six

Website
www.iSpeak4KidsGlobal.com

Author's Work:

Homeschool Gone Wild
Inspired Learning Through Living

Made in the USA
Monee, IL
16 July 2020